Costumes fo

Copyright © 1995 by Lynn Chang

All rights reserved. No part of this book may be reproduced without written permission from the Publisher.

Library of Congress Cataloging-in-Publication Data:
Chang, Lynn.
    Costumes for your cat / by Lynn Chang.
        p.   cm.
    ISBN 0-8118-1029-1
    1. Costume.   2. Cats—Equipment and supplies.   I. Title
TT633.C47   1994
741.5'973—dc 20   94-43166
                              CIP

Printed in Hong Kong

Book and cover design:

Lynn Chang

your C A T

by Lynn Chang

Distributed in Canada by Raincoast Books, 8680 Cambie Street, Vancouver, B.C., V6P 6M9

10 9 8 7 6 5 4 3 2 1

Chronicle Books 275 Fifth Street San Francisco, CA 94103

dedicated
to all
cats everywhere

with many thanks
to my family, friends,
Katharine, Charlotte
Uncle David and
especially
Sheefer

Table of Contents

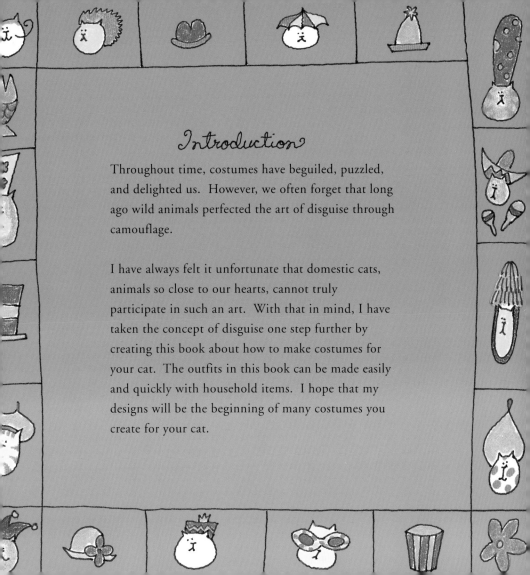

Introduction

Throughout time, costumes have beguiled, puzzled, and delighted us. However, we often forget that long ago wild animals perfected the art of disguise through camouflage.

I have always felt it unfortunate that domestic cats, animals so close to our hearts, cannot truly participate in such an art. With that in mind, I have taken the concept of disguise one step further by creating this book about how to make costumes for your cat. The outfits in this book can be made easily and quickly with household items. I hope that my designs will be the beginning of many costumes you create for your cat.

	KITTEN	JUVENILE	ADULT
Measuring Chart			
NECK			
HEAD WIDTH			
LEG LENGTH			
BODY LENGTH			
GIRTH			

This convenient measuring chart was developed so that you may make the costumes after just one fitting session. Cats tend to lose interest in these projects after their first fitting.

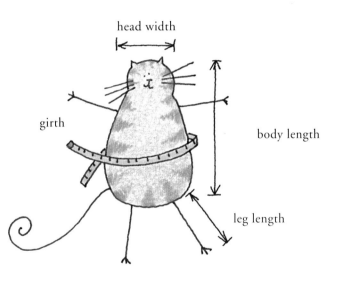

head width

girth

body length

leg length

scissors

glue

hole punch

straight pins

needle & thread

ruler

CHAPTER 1

Holidays

Throughout the year, holidays provide excitement for everyone. What better way to let your cat share in the fun than to dress him or her up in festive costumes?

New Year's Kitten

So simple, yet so effective.

THINGS YOU NEED

1 cloth diaper
2 safety pins

DIRECTIONS

1. Fold diaper in half, lengthwise. Cut hole for tail, as shown.

2. Roll sides of diaper in, as shown, and pinch in sides.

3. Lay diaper flat on ground and place cat belly up on it.
   Pull tail through hole. Wrap diaper snugly around
   cat's waist and pin at each side.

Thanksgiving Cat

Your cat will thank you for this one.

THINGS YOU NEED

1 piece of pink bubblegum
1 sheet of earth tone construction paper
1 package of color pencils
1 5" length of elastic

DIRECTIONS

1. Unwrap piece of gum and chew during preparation.

2. Accordion fold paper into strips.

3. Draw feather shape on top strip; cut along lines through all thicknesses, taking care not to cut through bottom so feathers stay together.

4. Fringe edges as shown. Unfold.

5. Decorate with pencils. Punch holes on edges; fold up bottom edge.

6. Attach elastic.

7. Wrap turkey tail around cat's girth.

8. Remove gum from mouth, pulling slightly and press one end of sticky gum to cat's chin.

Easter Bunny

This never fails to get your cat hippety-hopping down that trail.

THINGS YOU NEED

1 piece of white cardboard
1 pink pencil
1 15" length of pink ribbon
1 12" length of string
1 large cotton ball
3 dyed eggs

DIRECTIONS

1. Fold cardboard in two. Draw bunny ear shape on curved band, as shown, and cut along line through all thicknesses.

2. Unfold. Color inside of ears pink. Punch holes on sides of band.

3. Cut ribbon in half. Attach one ribbon in each band hole.

4. Holding cat firmly, position ears on top of cat's head, and tie ribbon under chin.

5. Tie string tightly around cotton ball, then tie cotton ball to base of cat's tail. Fluff as necessary.

6. Arrange eggs around cat.

CHAPTER TWO

TALENT SHOW

Cats love attention. Why else do they stay up all
night and sing love songs or sit on your papers while
you work? This chapter best reflects your cat's
desire to be at center stage.

Modern Dance

Expressive movement for today's contemporary cat.

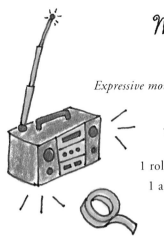

THINGS YOU NEED

1 roll of glow-in-the-dark tape
1 alternative-music cassette
stereo or boom box

DIRECTIONS

Hint: For best results, try this one at night.

1. Cut approximately twenty one-inch
   pieces of tape.

2. Holding cat, stick tape pieces on
   cat's body in thought-provoking patterns.

3. Turn on alternative music.

4. Turn out lights; let go of cat.

One Cat Band

With this costume, your cat will be a hit at any party.

THINGS YOU NEED

4 small pie tins
8 5" lengths of elastic
4 jingle bells
1 coat hanger
1 harmonica
1 can of fresh cat food

DIRECTIONS

1. Punch two holes in each tin plate. Using one elastic per plate, run an elastic piece through each hole; tie ends, leaving enough space for cat's legs.

2. Attach jingle bells to remaining pieces of elastic, again leaving enough space for cat's legs.

3. Bend coat hanger as shown and place around cat's neck.

4. Place harmonica in the makeshift holder. Adjust so that harmonica presses against cat's lips.

5. Loop tins around cat's knees and attach bells around each ankle.

6. Open can of cat food at opposite end of room.

Tap Dance Kitty

Let your cat relive those glamorous Hollywood days.

THINGS YOU NEED

4 5" x 5" pieces of aluminum foil
1 45" x 8" piece of gold lamé fabric
1 spool of gold thread
1 24" length of silver ribbon

DIRECTIONS

1. Cut foil into four 5" x 5" pieces. Set aside.

2. Hem edges of fabric, as shown.

3. Fold fabric with wrong sides together; stitch through all thicknesses.
   Turn inside out.
   Press flat.

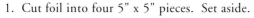

4. Stitch through all thicknesses once more, 3/4" from sewn edge, to form casing. Insert ribbon through casing.
   Gather material and tack bottom edge, as shown.

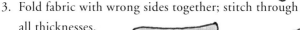

5. Tie collar around cat's neck.

6. Wrap pieces of foil into firm balls on each paw.

7. Place cat on top of an uncarpeted staircase.

PERIOD COSTUMES

CHAPTER III

With a little imagination, your cat can experience
the wonderful history of fashion.

Cave Cat

Bring your cat back to his or her feline origins.

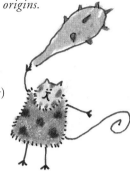

THINGS YOU NEED

2 12" x 12" pieces of fake fur
(preferably saber-toothed tiger)
1 48" length of string
spiky club (optional)

DIRECTIONS

1. Draw costume shape on back of each piece of fur,
   as shown. Cut along dotted lines.

male cat   female cat

2. Sew sides with string, leaving armhole(s) open,
   as indicated. Sew across tops of pieces, leaving
   edges unfinished.

3. Pull over cat and adjust as necessary.

4. Accessorize with spiky club.

Elizabethan Cat

A regal fantasy for the aristocratic cat.

THINGS YOU NEED

1 6" x 120" piece of stiff white paper
1 24" length of lavender ribbon

DIRECTIONS

1. Accordion fold paper, as shown.

2. Punch hole at top center through all thicknesses of paper.
   Pass ribbon through hole.

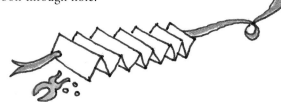

3. Wrap paper accordion around cat's neck, adjust folds,
   and tie bow at back.

1970's Hip Cat

For every cat with soul.

THINGS YOU NEED

1 8" length of elastic
1 ball lime green or purple sparkle mohair
peace pendant on 7" gold chain
Saturday Night Fever video

DIRECTIONS

1. Sew elastic into loop (check head width on measuring chart).

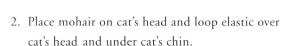

2. Place mohair on cat's head and loop elastic over cat's head and under cat's chin.

3. Place pendant around cat's neck.

4. Watch *Saturday Night Fever* with cat.

Chapter Four

SOCK COSTUMES

Don't throw away those unmatched socks or
old pantyhose! They will be useful for the
unforgettable costumes on the following pages.

Elephant Walking Backwards

A personal favorite with a touch of safari.

THINGS YOU NEED

1 12" x 12" square of gray felt
1 12" x 12" square of white felt
1 sock, preferably a solid color
2 black 1/2" – 5/8" buttons

DIRECTIONS

1. Fold each square of felt in half. Draw and cut out ear and tusk shapes from gray and white felt, as shown.

2. Sew an ear on each side of sock and glue tusks slightly below ears.

3. Sew buttons on as eyes.

4. Place sock gently, but firmly, over cat's head and watch the elephant walk backwards.

Caterpillar

A complex costume, but worth the effort.

THINGS YOU NEED

3 extra-large socks
2 pipe cleaners
2 pom-poms

DIRECTIONS

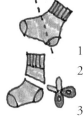

1. Cut tops of two socks off, as shown. Set top pieces aside.
2. Cut toe portion of socks down the middle to the toe.
   Press both pieces open.
3. Stitch pieces together forming a large casing.
   Cut four leg holes, as shown, on one side of casing.

4. To form caterpillar legs, cut top of each sock piece into five long strips.
   Fold in half widthwise and stitch along each side.
   Sew legs onto each side of large casing.

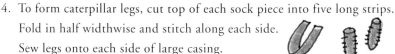

5. Bend pipe cleaners slightly and glue pom-poms on ends.
   Sew bent pipe cleaners to front and back of outfit, as shown.
6. Pull entire casing over cat, fitting legs through leg holes.

Cat Burglar

A cunning costume indeed.

THINGS YOU NEED

1 piece of 12" x 12" canvas
1 30" length of 30 lb. strength cotton cord
1 pair of pantyhose

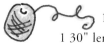

DIRECTIONS

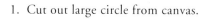

1. Cut out large circle from canvas.

2. Cut or punch holes around perimeter of canvas circle 1" apart.

3. Weave cord through holes.
   Draw loot bag tight, leaving 15" length on each end of cord.

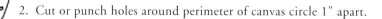

4. Tie loot bag to cat by looping cord across cat's chest in a
   criss-cross fashion, tying ends together at back.

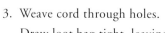

5. Cut off one foot of pantyhose, approximately 6" in length.

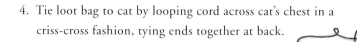

6. Stretch nylon foot snugly over cat's head. Expect resistance.

Chapter Five

T.V. EXTRAVAGANZA

The average cat spends hundreds of hours sleeping in front of or on the TV. Let your cat become the star of his or her favorite shows with these costume classics.

I Love Lucy

A costume so endearing, Lucille Ball would be proud.

THINGS YOU NEED

1 10" x 10" piece of red construction paper
1 jar of sparkle sprinkles
1 bag of cotton candy

DIRECTIONS

1. Fold paper in half. Cut out heart shape and a hole in the center of the heart for the head, as shown; cut twelve 1/2" slits around head hole for easier fitting.

2. On heart write "I Love Lucy" in script with white glue. Pour sprinkles over glue and allow to dry. Shake off excess sprinkles.

3. Place paper heart over cat's head.

4. Moisten cotton candy until slightly tacky. Stick on top of cat's head.

5. Sing theme song to *I Love Lucy*.

Chips

An ideal costume for the macho cat.

THINGS YOU NEED

1 5" x 5" piece of cardboard
1 5" length of elastic
1 mineral water spritzer
1 bottle of mousse and a blow dryer
1 pair of children's mirrored sunglasses
toy gun & holster

DIRECTIONS

1. Fold cardboard in half. Cut out badge shape, as shown.
2. Write "CHiPs" on top of badge and "Cat Highway Patrol" underneath. Draw cat face and palm tree details at each side, as shown.
3. Punch holes on sides of badge. Run elastic through each hole, knot ends, tying loose ends together.
4. Mist cat with spritzer until damp; liberally apply mousse and blow-dry cat's fur away from cat's face and body.
5. Rest sunglasses on cat's nose, strap holster around cat's waist, and loop badge around cat's right front leg.

Star Trek

A must for Trekkies.

THINGS YOU NEED

1 sq. yd. of light blue jersey

black iron-on knee patch

1 2" x 4" piece of cardboard

1 5" length of elastic

DIRECTIONS

1. Fold jersey in half. Cut out pattern, as shown, taking measurements from measuring chart.

2. Sew with wrong sides together, leaving neck and armholes open. Turn inside out and press. Roll down collar for mock turtleneck effect.

body length + 1⅛"

neck 1⅛

4"

½ girth + 1

3. Cut emblem out of iron-on patch. Iron on emblem to left front of jersey.

4. Decorate cardboard phasar. Punch out holes on sides; run elastic through holes and knot ends.

5. Pull jersey over cat's head; force front legs through armholes.

6. Strap phasar to front right leg of cat.

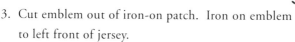